I0416739

HAYLEY HAYES

Navigating the Digital Landscape

Contents

1

The Foundations of Digital Marketing

Digital marketing has revolutionized the way businesses connect with consumers and promote their products or services. In this chapter, we will explore the fundamental principles and strategies that form the building blocks of successful digital marketing.

1. What is Digital Marketing?

Digital marketing encompasses all advertising and promotional efforts conducted through digital channels, such as websites, social media, email, search engines, and mobile applications. It leverages technology to reach and engage with target audiences in a more personalized and interactive manner.

In today's digital landscape, consumers spend an increasing amount of time online, making digital marketing an essential component of any comprehensive marketing strategy. By harnessing the power of digital channels, businesses can effectively communicate with their target audience, build brand awareness, drive conversions, and ultimately achieve business growth.

2. The Evolution of Digital Marketing

Since the advent of the internet, digital marketing has evolved significantly, adapting to changes in technology and consumer behavior. From the early days of banner ads and email marketing to the rise of social media and content marketing, the industry has witnessed numerous transformations.

One of the major drivers of this evolution is the changing consumer behavior spurred by technological advancements. Consumers now have easy access to information, research capabilities, and multiple channels for engaging with brands. Businesses have had to adapt to this shift by adopting digital strategies that allow them to connect with their target audience, deliver personalized experiences, and foster meaningful relationships.

3. Key Components of a Digital Marketing Strategy

To succeed in the digital realm, it is essential to have a clear and comprehensive strategy. This involves defining your goals, identifying your target audience, selecting the right digital channels, creating compelling content, and measuring the effectiveness of your efforts.

Defining goals: Every digital marketing campaign should start with clearly defined goals. Whether it's increasing brand awareness, driving website traffic, generating leads, or boosting sales, establishing specific and measurable objectives ensures a focused strategy.

Identifying target audience: Understanding the characteristics, preferences, and needs of your target audience is crucial for effective digital marketing. Conducting market research, analyzing consumer data, and developing buyer personas can help refine your messaging, channel selection, and content creation.

Digital channel selection: With so many digital channels available, it is important to select the ones that align with your target audience and goals. Websites, search engines, social media platforms, email marketing, mobile applications, and other emerging technologies each have unique attributes and offer various opportunities for engagement.

Compelling content creation: Content is the driving force behind successful digital marketing efforts. Creating relevant, high-quality content that connects with your audience is essential for building trust, establishing thought leadership, and driving conversions. From blog articles and social media posts to videos and interactive experiences, choosing the right content formats and mediums is key.

Measuring effectiveness: Measuring the impact of your digital marketing activities is crucial for optimizing your strategy and allocating resources effectively. Utilizing analytics tools, tracking key metrics, and conducting regular performance evaluations will help you identify areas for improvement and make data-driven decisions.

4. Understanding the Digital Consumer

Understanding the behavior and preferences of the digital consumer is crucial for effective digital marketing. By gaining insights into their online habits, preferences, and motivations, businesses can tailor their marketing efforts to provide a more personalized and relevant experience.

Demographics and psychographics: Defining and understanding the demographics (age, gender, location, etc.) and psychographics (interests, values, lifestyle) of your target audience is the foundation of successful marketing. These factors help shape your messaging, creative elements, and channel selection.

Online behavior: Observation and analysis of online behavior can provide valuable insights into consumer preferences, decision-making processes, and purchasing patterns. Utilizing tools like website analytics, heat maps, and social listening can help businesses understand how consumers interact with their digital assets.

Consumer journey mapping: Mapping the customer journey helps identify touchpoints and interactions throughout their decision-making process. Recognizing the stages of awareness, consideration, and decision-making allows businesses to deliver the right messages and experiences at each step, effectively guiding consumers toward conversion.

Consumer engagement: Successful digital marketing involves fostering engagement and building relationships with consumers. By leveraging social media, email marketing, chatbots, and other interactive technologies, businesses can create opportunities for dialogue, listen to customer feedback, and provide personalized experiences.

5. Building Brand Awareness and Online Presence

Establishing a strong online presence is essential for any business aiming to thrive in the digital age. This involves creating a visually appealing and user-friendly website that provides a seamless experience across all devices.

Website design and optimization: A well-designed website serves as the centerpiece of a brand's online presence. Optimizing the website for search engines using techniques such as on-page optimization, content optimization, and responsive design ensures better visibility and user experience.

Search engine presence: Increasing visibility in search engine results is vital for driving organic traffic to your website. Employing search engine optimization (SEO) techniques, businesses can improve their website's ranking by targeting relevant keywords, optimizing meta tags, building quality backlinks, and creating valuable content.

Social media engagement: Social media platforms play a crucial role in building brand awareness and engaging with target audiences. Strategic use of social media marketing techniques such as content curation, influencer partnerships, community building, and paid advertising can amplify brand messaging, spark conversations, and drive website traffic.

6. The Role of Content Marketing

Content marketing has emerged as a powerful strategy in the digital marketing landscape. It involves creating and sharing valuable, informative, and engaging content that resonates with the target audience.

Content strategy: A well-defined content strategy ensures that businesses consistently create and distribute compelling content that aligns with their brand goals and resonates with their audience. Content strategy encompasses content planning, production, distribution, and analysis.

Types of content: Content comes in various formats, including blog posts, articles, infographics, videos, podcasts, and social media posts. Choosing the right format depends on the target audience's preferences, the message being conveyed, and the desired impact.

Personalization: Personalized content is key to capturing the attention of consumers in a digital landscape filled with noise. By leveraging data and consumer insights, businesses can deliver tailored content experiences that address individual needs, pain points, and interests.

Storytelling: Storytelling is a powerful technique within content marketing. By crafting narratives that evoke emotions, connect with values, and create memorable experiences, businesses can effectively engage with their audience and differentiate themselves from competitors.

7. Search Engine Optimization (SEO)

Search engine optimization is the process of optimizing a website to rank higher in search engine results pages. By employing various SEO techniques, businesses can increase their visibility, drive organic traffic, and improve their chances of being discovered by potential customers.

Keyword research: Conducting keyword research enables businesses to identify the terms and phrases their target audience uses when searching for products or services. By strategically incorporating these keywords into their website content, businesses optimize their chances of ranking higher in search results.

On-page optimization: On-page optimization focuses on optimizing various elements on web pages, such as meta tags, headings, URLs, image alt tags, and content structure. By following SEO best practices, businesses can improve their website's relevance, user experience, and search engine visibility.

Technical optimization: Technical SEO. Technical optimization: Technical SEO involves optimizing the technical aspects of a website to ensure that search engines can crawl and index it effectively. This includes factors such as website speed, mobile-friendliness, site structure, XML sitemaps, and canonical tags. By addressing technical issues and implementing best practices, businesses can improve their website's search engine ranking.

Link building: Link building refers to the process of acquiring high-quality backlinks from other websites. Search engines consider backlinks as a vote of confidence in a site's credibility and authority. By actively building relationships, creating valuable content, and promoting their website, businesses can increase the number of reputable backlinks they receive, enhancing their search engine visibility.

Local SEO: For businesses targeting local customers, local SEO is crucial.

Optimizing for local search involves optimizing the website for location-specific keywords, creating and optimizing a Google My Business profile, getting positive customer reviews, and ensuring consistency in NAP (Name, Address, Phone Number) citations across various online directories.

8. Pay-Per-Click (PPC) Advertising

Pay-per-click advertising is a digital marketing model in which advertisers pay each time their ad is clicked. This approach allows businesses to display ads on search engines, social media platforms, or other websites and only pay when a user takes a specific action, such as clicking on the ad or making a purchase.

Search Engine Advertising: Search engine advertising, also known as search ads or paid search, involves bidding on keywords and creating text-based ads that appear at the top of search engine results pages. Advertisers pay a fee each time a user clicks on their ad.

Display Advertising: Display advertising involves placing visual ads, such as banners or rich media ads, on websites, apps, or social media platforms. Advertisers can target specific audiences based on demographics, interests, or online behavior.

Social Media Advertising: Social media platforms offer robust advertising capabilities, allowing businesses to target specific demographics and interests. With options such as sponsored posts, carousel ads, and video ads, businesses can promote their products or services and engage with their target audience.

Remarketing: Remarketing involves targeting ads to users who have previously visited your website or engaged with your brand. By using tracking pixels or cookies, businesses can display targeted ads to these users as they browse other websites or social media platforms, increasing the chances of conversion.

9. Email Marketing

Email marketing is a direct form of digital marketing that involves sending targeted promotional messages or newsletters to a subscriber list. When done effectively, email marketing can drive customer engagement, foster loyalty, and generate conversions.

Building an email list: To conduct email marketing campaigns, businesses need to build an email list of interested subscribers. This can be done by offering incentives, such as lead magnets or discounts, and utilizing opt-in forms on websites or social media platforms.

Email automation and segmentation: Email marketing platforms offer automation and segmentation capabilities, allowing businesses to send personalized emails based on specific triggers or criteria. By segmenting their email list based on demographics, purchase history, or engagement level, businesses can ensure their messages are relevant and targeted.

Personalization and customization: Personalization is the key to successful email marketing. By addressing subscribers by name, tailoring content based on their preferences and interests, and utilizing dynamic content, businesses can create personalized experiences that resonate with their audience.

Tracking and analytics: Email marketing platforms provide analytics and tracking features that allow businesses to monitor the performance of their email campaigns. By tracking metrics such as open rates, click-through rates, and conversions, businesses can optimize their email marketing strategy and improve their results over time.

10. The Mobile Experience

In today's digital landscape, it is essential for businesses to optimize their digital marketing efforts for mobile devices. With the majority of online interactions now happening on smartphones and tablets, businesses need to ensure that their websites and digital assets are mobile-friendly and provide a seamless user experience.

Responsive design: Responsive web design ensures that a website adapts to different screen sizes and devices, providing a consistent and optimized experience for users. This eliminates the need for separate mobile and desktop websites and allows businesses to reach their audience regardless of the device they are using.

Mobile app marketing: For businesses with mobile applications, mobile app marketing plays a crucial role in promoting and driving engagement with their app. This involves optimizing the app store listing, implementing in-app marketing strategies, and utilizing push notifications to engage with users.

Mobile advertising: Mobile advertising involves creating ads that are specifically designed for mobile devices and utilizing mobile-specific ad formats, such as interstitial ads or in-app advertisements. Businesses can leverage location-based targeting and mobile user behavior data to deliver personalized and relevant ads to mobile users.

Mobile optimization: In addition to responsive design, businesses need to ensure that their digital assets, such as landing pages, forms, and emails, are optimized for mobile devices. This includes minimizing load times, streamlining navigation, and using mobile-friendly formats and buttons.

In conclusion, digital marketing is an ever-evolving field that requires businesses to adapt to changing consumer behavior and technological advancements. By understanding the key components of a digital marketing strategy, the behavior of the digital consumer, and implementing tactics such as content marketing, SEO, PPC advertising, email marketing, and mobile optimization, businesses can effectively connect with their target audience, drive engagement, and achieve their marketing goals.

2

Understanding the Digital Consumer

In today's rapidly evolving digital landscape, understanding the complexities of the modern digital consumer has become paramount for marketers. The rise of technology and the internet has revolutionized the way people interact, shop, and consume information. As a result, marketers need to adapt their strategies to meet the changing expectations and preferences of the digital consumer.

One of the key aspects of understanding the digital consumer is recognizing their deep reliance on technology as a means of communication, research, and entertainment. With the widespread adoption of smartphones, tablets, and other connected devices, consumers now have constant access to the internet. This has fundamentally changed the way they make purchasing decisions, as they can effortlessly compare products, read reviews, and seek recommendations from their social networks. The ability to access information at the touch of a button has empowered consumers and transformed their role in the buying process.

Furthermore, the digital consumer has become more demanding and discerning in their choices of brands to engage with. They expect personalized experiences, tailored content, and seamless interactions across multiple channels. Marketers need to leverage data and technology to gain insights into their target audience and deliver relevant and engaging experiences. By utilizing customer data and employing strategies like segmentation and targeting, marketers can create personalized messages that resonate with individual consumers. This level of personalization helps build meaningful connections and, in turn, fosters brand loyalty.

Social media platforms have also played a significant role in shaping the behavior of the digital consumer. Consumers now have the power to voice their opinions, share experiences, and influence others through these channels. This social proof has become a valuable asset for brands, as positive reviews and word-of-mouth recommendations can significantly impact purchasing decisions. Social media has also given rise to influencer marketing, where individuals with large followings endorse products or services, thereby influencing the perception and purchasing decisions of their audience. Brands that can effectively tap into the power of social media by engaging with customers, addressing concerns, and fostering a sense of community are more likely to succeed in this digital era.

Additionally, the digital consumer craves authenticity and transparency from the brands they choose to support. They want to understand the values and purpose behind a brand and connect with its story. Companies that can successfully convey their brand identity and build trust with their audience are more likely to thrive in the digital era. This requires consistent messaging and aligning brand values with customer expectations. Consumers are increasingly drawn to brands that are socially responsible, environmentally conscious, and actively engaged in giving back to society. Brands that can authentically communicate their commitment to these values are more likely to resonate with consumers and win their loyalty.

As technology continues to advance, the digital consumer is also increasingly concerned about privacy and data security. With the increasing amount of personal information shared online, consumers are wary of how their data is being collected, stored, and used. Brands that prioritize data security and communicate transparently about their data practices can build trust with their customers and differentiate themselves from competitors.

Another significant aspect of understanding the digital consumer is recognizing the shift in their media consumption habits. Traditional media channels, such as television and radio, have lost some of their dominance, as consumers now prefer consuming content on-demand through streaming services, podcasts, and social media platforms. This has led to an increase in ad-blocking software and the rise of ad-free subscription models. To effectively reach the digital consumer, marketers need to understand their preferred channels and create compelling content that aligns with their interests and values.

Furthermore, the digital consumer is increasingly embracing convenience and seamless experiences. With the growth of the e-commerce industry, consumers now expect fast shipping, easy returns, and hassle-free shopping experiences. Voice assistants, such as Amazon's Alexa and Google Assistant, have also gained popularity, enabling consumers to make purchases with just a few voice commands. Marketers need to optimize their online platforms and embrace emerging technologies like artificial intelligence and chatbots to provide seamless and efficient customer experiences.

To truly understand the digital consumer, marketers must continually adapt and stay informed about the latest trends and technologies that shape their behavior. This could involve conducting market research, utilizing analytics tools, and staying up-to-date with industry news and insights. By doing so, marketers can tailor their strategies to better align with consumer expectations and engage with them in meaningful ways.

In conclusion, understanding the digital consumer is crucial for marketers looking to thrive in the digital age. By recognizing their deep reliance on technology, their demand for personalized experiences, their influence on social media, their desire for authentic brand engagements, and their concerns about privacy and data security, marketers can effectively connect with their target audience and drive meaningful results in the digital landscape. Through continuous adaptation and understanding of consumer behavior, marketers can unlock the full potential of today's digital consumer and create long-lasting, mutually beneficial relationships.

3

Creating a Digital Marketing Strategy

A digital marketing strategy is the backbone of every successful online business. It provides a roadmap for achieving marketing goals and objectives in the digital realm. In this chapter, we will dive deeper into the process of creating a comprehensive and effective digital marketing strategy, equipping you with the knowledge and tools needed to succeed in the competitive online landscape.

1. Understand Your Target Audience:

To create an effective digital marketing strategy, it is crucial to have a deep understanding of your target audience. Start by developing buyer personas - fictional representations of your ideal customers. Gather data through research, surveys, and customer feedback to define their demographics, preferences, and pain points. Understanding your audience's motivations, needs, and behaviors will help you tailor your strategy to resonate with them effectively.

Furthermore, it's essential to conduct market research and competitive analysis to gain insights into your industry and identify your unique selling proposition (USP). By studying your competitors, you can identify gaps in the market and refine your strategy to set yourself apart. Analyze your competitors' digital presence, messaging, and marketing tactics to learn from their successes and failures.

2. Set Clear and Measurable Goals:

Goals are fundamental to any marketing strategy. They provide direction, focus, and a means of measuring success. Set specific, measurable, achievable, relevant, and time-bound (SMART) goals that align with your business objectives. For example, your goals could include increasing website traffic by 20%, achieving a 15% conversion rate on landing pages, or generating 500 qualified leads per month. Clear and measurable goals will keep you and your team focused and motivated.

To ensure your goals are realistic and ambitious, consider your available resources, budget, and timeline. Break down your goals into smaller milestones and establish key performance indicators (KPIs) to track progress.

3. Evaluate Your Online Presence:

Conducting a comprehensive analysis of your current online presence is critical to understanding your strengths, weaknesses, and areas for improvement. This analysis should cover your website, social media channels, email marketing campaigns, online advertising efforts, and any other relevant digital platforms you use.

Evaluate your website by examining its design, user experience, and overall functionality. Is your website mobile-friendly and optimized for search engines? Assess the quality and relevance of your website content, ensuring it aligns with your target audience's informational needs and search intent. Improve your website's load speed, navigation, and next steps to enhance the user experience and drive conversions.

Analyze your social media channels, considering the engagement rates, follower growth, and the effectiveness of your content strategy. Identify which social media platforms your target audience frequents and focus your efforts there. Develop a consistent brand voice and messaging across your social media channels to strengthen brand recognition.

Review your email marketing campaigns, assessing open rates, click-through rates, and unsubscribe rates. Ensure your email content is valuable, personalized, and aligned with the buyer's journey. Segment your email lists to deliver targeted messages that resonate with specific audience segments.

Evaluate your online advertising efforts, such as pay-per-click (PPC) campaigns and display ads. Analyze their return on ad spend (ROAS), click-through rates (CTR), and conversion rates. Optimize your ad copy, landing pages, and targeting parameters to improve performance.

4. Select the Right Digital Marketing Channels:

Choosing the right digital marketing channels to reach your target audience is essential. It's important to understand the characteristics and advantages of different channels to determine which align best with your goals and audience.

Search Engine Optimization (SEO): Enhancing your website's visibility in organic search results is crucial for driving relevant traffic. Optimize your website by conducting keyword research, developing high-quality content, improving site architecture, and building authoritative backlinks.

Pay-Per-Click (PPC) Advertising: Placing ads on search engines and websites allows you to appear at the top of search results and on relevant websites. Develop targeted campaigns, conduct keyword research, and optimize your ad copy and landing pages to maximize conversions.

Social Media Marketing: Leveraging popular social media platforms such as Facebook, Instagram, Twitter, LinkedIn, and YouTube can help you engage with your audience, build brand awareness, and drive traffic. Develop a social media strategy that aligns with your audience's preferences and behaviors. Create compelling and shareable content, interact with your followers, and utilize social media advertising options to expand your reach.

Content Marketing: Creating valuable and relevant content, such as blog posts, videos, and infographics, is vital for attracting and retaining your audience. Develop a content strategy that addresses your audience's pain points, educates and entertains them, and establishes your authority in the industry. Promote your content through social media, email marketing, and influencer collaborations.

Email Marketing: Utilize targeted email campaigns to nurture leads, build relationships, and drive conversions. Segment your email lists based on characteristics and behaviors. Develop personalized and impactful emails to provide value to your subscribers and guide them through the buyer's journey.

Influencer Partnerships: Collaborate with industry influencers or micro-influencers to expand your reach and tap into their engaged audiences. Identify influencers who align with your brand values and target audience. Develop authentic and mutually beneficial partnerships that leverage the influencer's influence and creativity to promote your products or services.

Consider your audience's preferences, behaviors, and the nature of your business when selecting channels. A multi-channel approach is often effective to reach a broader audience and maximize visibility. However, it's essential to focus your efforts and resources where they will have the most impact.

5. Create a Detailed Action Plan:

Having identified the most suitable channels, it's time to develop a detailed action plan. Outline the specific tactics, strategies, and activities you will undertake to achieve your marketing goals. This plan should include timelines, budgets, and responsibilities for each task or initiative.

For example, if your goal is to increase website traffic by 20%, your action plan may include activities such as optimizing your website's SEO, creating and promoting high-quality content, running PPC campaigns, and engaging with influencers. Assign tasks to team members, set deadlines, and establish a budget for each initiative.

It's also crucial to establish key performance indicators (KPIs) for each channel and tactic to track progress towards your goals. Monitor and review the performance of your campaigns regularly and adjust your strategy as needed.

6. Implement, Monitor, and Analyze:

Once your action plan is in place, start implementing your digital marketing strategies across the selected channels. Execute your tactics using the allocated resources, tools, and technologies. Maintain proactive communication within your team to ensure everyone is aligned and working towards the common goals.

Monitor the performance of your campaigns and initiatives by tracking key metrics. Utilize tools like Google Analytics, social media analytics, and marketing automation platforms to measure and analyze metrics such as website traffic, conversion rates, engagement levels, return on ad spend (ROAS), customer acquisition cost (CAC), and customer lifetime value (CLTV).

Conduct A/B testing on your campaigns to identify what works best for your target audience. Test variations of ad copy, landing page designs, email subject lines, and content formats. Use data-driven insights to optimize your digital marketing efforts continuously.

Analyzing your digital marketing results helps identify successful strategies and areas for improvement. Regularly review these insights to refine your approach and make data-backed decisions for future campaigns.

7. Refine and AdaptRefine and Adapt Your Strategy:

Digital marketing is a dynamic field, and it's important to regularly evaluate and refine your strategy to stay ahead of the competition. Use the insights gained from your monitoring and analysis to identify areas that are performing well and those that need improvement.

Optimize underperforming campaigns by making adjustments to targeting, messaging, and creative elements. Experiment with different strategies and tactics to find what resonates most with your audience. Continuously update and improve your content, website, and social media profiles to stay fresh and relevant.

Stay up to date with industry trends, consumer preferences, and changes in technology and algorithms. Attend industry conferences, participate in webinars, and join relevant online communities to stay informed and learn from others in your field.

Be open to trying new channels or technologies that can enhance your digital marketing efforts. For example, you might consider incorporating emerging technologies like artificial intelligence (AI) and chatbots into your customer service and communication strategies.

Constantly assess the competition to understand what they are doing well and identify opportunities for differentiation. Identify gaps in the market that you can fill and develop strategies to capture those opportunities.

Stay connected with your audience by actively engaging with them through social media, responding to comments and messages, and seeking feedback. Regularly gather customer insights and apply them to refine your communication, targeting, and product or service offerings.

Creating a comprehensive and effective digital marketing strategy requires a deep understanding of your target audience, clear and measurable goals, a thorough evaluation of your online presence, careful selection of the right digital marketing channels, a detailed action plan, implementation, monitoring, analysis, and constant refinement.

By following these steps and adapting to the ever-changing digital landscape, you can develop a strategy that not only reaches your target audience but also engages them, builds brand loyalty, and drives conversions. With a well-executed digital marketing strategy, your business can thrive in the competitive digital marketplace.

4

Building and Optimizing Websites for Success

In today's digital age, having a well-built and optimized website is crucial for the success of your business. A website is often the first point of contact for potential customers, and it needs to make a strong first impression. In this chapter, we will explore the key elements of building and optimizing websites to ensure that they not only attract visitors but also convert them into customers.

1. Understanding Your Target Audience:

To build an effective website, start by understanding your target audience. Conduct thorough market research to identify their demographics, preferences, needs, and pain points. This knowledge will help you tailor your website's design, content, and functionality to meet their specific expectations.

Demographics: Gather data on your target audience's age, gender, location, education level, income, and other relevant factors. This information will influence the overall look and feel of your website.

User Personas: Create fictional representations of different user segments to better understand their motivations, challenges, and goals. This will help you design content that resonates with their needs.

2. User-Friendly Design:

A cluttered and confusing website design can discourage visitors from exploring further. Aim for a clean and intuitive design by following these principles:

Clear Navigation: Organize your website's menu and internal links logically, making it easy for visitors to find what they're looking for. Use descriptive labels that align with users' mental models and include a search function if applicable.

Consistent Layout: Maintain a consistent design throughout your website to provide a cohesive and professional look. Consistency in colors, fonts, buttons, and other elements creates a seamless user experience.

Visual Hierarchy: Use headings, subheadings, and appropriate font sizes to guide visitors' attention and emphasize important information. Employ white space strategically to increase readability and highlight key elements.

Intuitive User Experience (UX): Create a seamless journey for users by optimizing the flow from one page to another, ensuring easy access to vital information. Conduct usability tests to identify pain points and address them promptly.

3. Search Engine Optimization (SEO):

SEO is essential for improving your website's visibility in search engine results. Here are some key strategies to optimize your website for search engines:

Keyword Research: Identify relevant keywords and incorporate them naturally within your website's content, meta descriptions, headings, and URLs. Use tools like Google Keyword Planner, SEMrush, or Moz Keyword Explorer to discover keywords with high search volume and low competition.

High-Quality Content: Produce valuable, informative content that incorporates relevant keywords to increase your website's organic visibility. Invest in a content marketing strategy that aligns with your target audience's interests and pain points.

On-Page Optimization: Ensure that your website's meta tags, title tags, and alt tags are optimized to accurately describe your content to search engines.

Optimize your URLs by making them concise, descriptive, and keyword-rich.

4. Fast Loading Speed:

A slow-loading website can drive visitors away. Utilize these techniques to improve your website's loading speed:

Image Optimization: Compress and resize images without compromising their quality to reduce file sizes. Use image formats like JPEG or WebP for photographs and PNG for graphics or images with transparency.

Minimize Redirects: Limit the number of redirects on your website as they increase loading time. Regularly check and update broken links to maintain a smooth user experience.

Caching: Utilize browser caching to store static files, reducing the need for repeated downloads. Leverage content delivery networks (CDNs) to distribute your website's files and decrease latency.

5. Mobile Optimization:

Given the rise in mobile internet usage, it's vital to optimize your website for mobile devices. Consider the following:

Responsive Design: Create a website that adapts to different screen sizes, ensuring an optimal user experience across devices. Test your website across various devices and screen resolutions to ensure consistent functionality and aesthetics.

Mobile User Experience: Make navigation easy, use large text and buttons, and minimize the need for zooming and scrolling. Prioritize important content and calls-to-action to provide a seamless mobile experience.

6. Website Security:

Protecting user data is crucial for maintaining trust. Implement the following security measures:

SSL Certificates: Obtain and install SSL certificates to encrypt data transmission and secure sensitive information. Users are more likely to trust websites that display the padlock symbol and "https" in the URL.

Regular Updates: Keep your website's software, plugins, and themes up-to-date to minimize vulnerabilities. Timely updates often include security patches, bug fixes, and performance improvements.

7. Performance Monitoring and Analysis:

Regularly track and measure your website's performance to identify areas for improvement. Utilize analytics tools to monitor metrics such as:

Traffic Sources: Determine where your visitors are coming from, enabling you to tailor marketing strategies accordingly. Analyze referral traffic, search traffic, and direct traffic to understand which channels are driving the most engagement.

Bounce Rates: Assess the percentage of visitors who leave your website without taking any further action. High bounce rates may indicate issues with website design, content, or user experience. Analyze specific pages with high bounce rates and optimize them to increase engagement.

Conversion Rates: Track the percentage of visitors who complete desired actions, such as making a purchase or filling out a form. By analyzing conversion rates, you can identify areas in need of optimization and run A/B tests to improve outcomes.

By implementing these strategies and continuously refining your website, you can create a powerful online presence that attracts and converts visitors into loyal customers. Remember, your website plays a central role in your digital marketing efforts, and prioritizing its optimization is essential for achieving long-term success in the competitive online landscape.

5

Search Engine Optimization (SEO) Essentials

In the ever-evolving digital landscape, having a strong online presence is crucial for businesses and brands alike. With a plethora of websites vying for attention, how can you ensure that your website stands out from the rest? That's where Search Engine Optimization (SEO) comes into the picture.

SEO is the practice of optimizing your website to improve its visibility and ranking on search engine results pages (SERPs). By incorporating strategic tactics, you can attract organic (unpaid) traffic and increase your chances of being found by users searching for relevant keywords. In this extended chapter, we will delve deeper into the world of SEO and explore additional strategies and techniques.

1. Keyword Research:

Keyword research is the foundation of any successful SEO campaign. It involves understanding the keywords your target audience searches for and tailoring your website's content to match their intent. Start by identifying core keywords related to your products or services. Then, use keyword research tools like Google Keyword Planner, SEMrush, or Ahrefs to discover high-volume keywords and long-tail variations.

Pay attention to search trends and user intent to ensure you optimize for the most relevant keywords in your industry. Look for keywords with high search volume and low competition. Long-tail keywords, which are more specific and longer phrases, can also bring in targeted traffic and have a higher chance of conversion.

2. On-Page Optimization:

On-page optimization involves optimizing the content and structure of your web pages to improve their search engine visibility. Start with the basics: ensure your website uses relevant keywords in page titles, headings, meta descriptions, and throughout the content. However, avoid keyword stuffing, as search engines penalize websites that engage in this practice.

Aim for natural and user-friendly language that provides value to your audience. Structure your content with headers (H1, H2, etc.) to improve readability and help search engines understand the hierarchy of information. Use descriptive URLs that include your target keywords. Make sure your web pages load quickly, as page speed is a ranking factor. Optimize images by compressing their size without losing quality and add descriptive alt text.

Additionally, create a logical and user-friendly navigation structure, allowing visitors to find what they're looking for quickly. Use internal linking to establish a strong information hierarchy and help search engines understand the relationships between your pages. This also encourages users to explore more of your content, improving engagement metrics.

3. Technical SEO:

Technical SEO focuses on optimizing the technical aspects of your website to improve its crawlability and indexability by search engines. Some important technical considerations include:

Site architecture and crawlability: Ensure your website has clean and crawlable code that search engine bots can easily navigate. Use a sitemap to provide search engines with an organized overview of your website's structure and content. Optimize your robots.txt file to control which areas of your website are accessible to search engine crawlers.

Duplicate content: Address issues with duplicate content, as search engines penalize websites that present identical or very similar content. Use canonical tags to indicate the preferred version of a page and implement 301 redirects for permanent URL changes.

Page speed: Optimize your website's loading speed, as slow-loading pages can negatively affect user experience and rankings. Compress images, leverage browser caching, minify CSS and JavaScript files, and reduce server response time.

Schema markup: Leverage schema markup (structured data) to provide search engines with additional context about your content. This enables rich snippets, which enhance your search engine listing with additional information and can improve your chances of being featured in knowledge graphs.

4. Off-Page Optimization:

Off-page optimization focuses on activities that improve your website's reputation, authority, and visibility outside of your own domain. Here are some effective off-page optimization techniques:

Link building: Build high-quality backlinks from authoritative and relevant websites. Earn backlinks naturally by creating high-quality, shareable content that people naturally want to link to. This can be achieved through content creation, guest posting, influencer outreach, and networking within your industry. Avoid low-quality or spammy backlinks, as they can harm your website's reputation.

Content marketing: Develop an engaging content marketing strategy that educates, informs, or entertains your target audience. Create valuable, shareable content that establishes you as an authoritative source in your industry. Promote your content through various channels, such as social media, email marketing, and outreach to influencers and industry leaders.

Social media promotion: Share your content on social media platforms to expand its reach and generate engagement. Use social media listening tools to monitor and engage with conversations related to your industry or brand. Encourage social sharing and foster a community around your brand.

Online PR: Develop relationships with journalists, bloggers, and online publications to secure coverage for your brand. Craft compelling press releases and pitch timely and newsworthy stories related to your industry. Participate in industry-related events and engage with relevant online communities to increase your visibility and authority.

5. User Experience and Mobile Optimization:

Search engines value websites that prioritize user experience. A seamless and user-friendly website not only keeps visitors engaged but also signals to search engines that your content is valuable. Pay attention to the following aspects:

Mobile optimization: As mobile usage continues to rise, it's essential that your website is responsive and mobile-friendly. Ensure that your website design adapts seamlessly to different screen sizes and resolutions. Implement AMP (Accelerated Mobile Pages) for a lightning-fast mobile experience.

Page load speeds: Improve your website's loading speed by optimizing images, leveraging browser caching, and minimizing unnecessary scripts. Users expect fast-loading pages, and search engines consider it a ranking factor. Regularly monitor and optimize your website's speed using tools like Google PageSpeed Insights or GTmetrix.

Featured snippets: Aim to optimize your content to appear in featured snippets, which provide direct answers to users' queries in search results. By structuring your content using headers and providing concise and informative answers, you increase the chances of being featured.

User engagement metrics: Monitor user engagement metrics, such as bounce rate, time on page, and pages per session. High bounce rates may indicate poor content relevance, slow loading speeds, or a confusing website structure. Analyze user behavior through heatmaps or session recordings to identify areas for improvement.

6. Continuous Monitoring and Analysis:

SEO is an ongoing process that requires continuous monitoring and analysis. By regularly assessing the performance of your SEO efforts, you can identify areas for improvement and adapt your strategies accordingly. Here are some essential metrics to track:

Organic traffic: Monitor the volume and quality of organic traffic to your website. Analyze which pages are driving the most traffic and whether visitors are engaging with your content. Use Google Analytics or other web analytics tools to gain insights into user behavior and traffic sources.

Keyword rankings: Regularly monitor your website's rankings for target keywords. Look for both improvements and declines, as they can help you uncover opportunities or address potential issues. Use keyword tracking tools like SEMrush or Moz to track your keyword positions and identify areas for improvement.

Conversion rates: Measure the effectiveness of your SEO efforts by tracking the conversion rates of visitors who complete desired actions, such as making a purchase, filling out a form, or subscribing to your newsletter. Set up conversion tracking in Google Analytics and optimize your website's conversion funnel to improve your conversion rates.

Backlink profile: Monitor the growth and quality of your backlink profile. Regularly check for new backlinks and evaluate their authority and relevance. Identify and address any toxic backlinks that may harm your website's reputation. Tools like Ahrefs or Moz can help you analyze and monitor your backlink profile.

Social signals: Track the engagement and reach of your content on social media platforms. Monitor metrics like shares, likes, comments, and followers. Analyze which types of content perform well on different social media channels and adjust your strategy accordingly.

Competitor analysis: Keep an eye on your competitors' SEO strategies and performance. Identify their top-ranking keywords, backlink sources, and content marketing strategies. Use this information to identify gaps and opportunities for your own website. By regularly monitoring and analyzing these metrics, you can make data-driven decisions and optimize your SEO strategies for better results.

In conclusion, Search Engine Optimization (SEO) is a dynamic and multifaceted practice that requires a combination of technical expertise, content creation, and ongoing analysis. By understanding and implementing the essential SEO techniques discussed in this chapter, you can improve your website's visibility, attract organic traffic, and ultimately grow your online presence. Stay up to date with the latest SEO trends and always prioritize the user experience to stay ahead of the competition and drive meaningful results for your business.

6

Pay-Per-Click (PPC) Advertising: Strategies and Techniques

Pay-Per-Click (PPC) advertising has become an essential component of any successful digital marketing strategy. With the ability to target specific audiences and track precise metrics, PPC advertising offers a cost-effective way to drive traffic and generate leads. In this chapter, we will explore the various platforms available for PPC advertising, including Facebook Ads, Google Ads, LinkedIn Ads, Instagram Ads, and YouTube Ads, along with strategies and techniques to maximize their effectiveness.

Facebook Ads:

Facebook Ads is a powerful platform that allows businesses to reach a massive audience of over 2 billion active users. The platform's sophisticated targeting options provide businesses with the opportunity to reach highly specific audiences based on demographics, interests, and behaviors. Through Facebook Ads, businesses can create ad campaigns targeting specific age groups, locations, interests, and even behaviors such as online shopping habits or past interactions with their website or app.

Facebook Ads offers a variety of ad formats to cater to different business objectives. Image ads are simple yet effective visuals that can display a product, offer, or brand message. Video ads allow businesses to tell a story or showcase their products through engaging videos. Carousel ads enable businesses to showcase multiple images or videos within a single ad, providing an opportunity to display a range of products or multiple features of a single product. Canvas ads are immersive and interactive experiences that allow businesses to create customized, full-screen mobile ads.

Google Ads:

Google Ads, formerly known as Google AdWords, is one of the most popular and widely used platforms for PPC advertising. By displaying ads on the top of search engine results pages, Google Ads allows businesses to reach potential customers who are actively searching for specific keywords. Keywords play a crucial role in Google Ads campaigns, as businesses need to select the right keywords to ensure their ads are shown to the most relevant audience.

Google Ads offers different campaign types to suit various marketing goals. Search Network campaigns show text ads on search engine results pages when users search for specific keywords. Display Network campaigns display visual ads on a network of websites, targeting users based on their browsing behavior and interests. Shopping campaigns showcase product ads with images and prices on Google's search results pages when users search for relevant keywords. Video campaigns enable businesses to display video ads on YouTube, reaching a vast audience of monthly users.

LinkedIn Ads:

LinkedIn Ads is an effective platform for businesses with a B2B focus, allowing them to reach professionals and decision-makers. With its emphasis on professional networking, LinkedIn offers targeting options based on job titles, industries, and company size. This specificity enables businesses to tailor their ad campaigns towards the LinkedIn audience by showcasing thought leadership content, industry-specific offerings, or career-related resources.

LinkedIn offers different ad formats, such as Sponsored Content, Sponsored InMail, and Text Ads, to effectively engage with the platform's professional user base. Sponsored Content appears directly in users' newsfeeds, allowing businesses to promote articles, blog posts, or other types of content to increase brand visibility and engagement. Sponsored InMail delivers personalized messages directly to users' LinkedIn inboxes, enabling businesses to deliver targeted messages to a specific audience. Text Ads are simple but effective text-based ads that appear on the right side of LinkedIn's desktop interface.

Instagram Ads:

Instagram Ads have become a valuable tool for businesses due to the platform's visually-driven nature and its integration with Facebook's advertising platform. With over 1 billion monthly active users, Instagram offers businesses the opportunity to showcase products and services in a visually appealing way. By utilizing eye-catching images, videos, and targeted hashtags, businesses can capture the attention of their target audience and drive engagement.

Instagram offers various ad formats, including photo ads, video ads, carousel ads, and story ads. Photo ads are simple yet effective visuals that can display a product, offer, or brand message. Video ads allow businesses to tell a story or showcase their products through engaging videos. Carousel ads enable businesses to showcase multiple images or videos within a single ad, providing an opportunity to display a range of products or multiple features of a single product. Story ads appear in Instagram Stories, a popular feature of the platform that allows businesses to create immersive and temporary visual content.

YouTube Ads:

As the largest video-sharing platform, YouTube provides businesses with the opportunity to reach a wide audience through video advertisements. With billions of monthly users, YouTube offers various ad formats, including skippable ads and non-skippable ads. Skippable ads allow viewers to skip the ad after a few seconds, while non-skippable ads must be watched in their entirety before the user can access the desired content.

Businesses can create compelling video content and use storytelling techniques to capture the attention of viewers and drive brand awareness and engagement. YouTube ads are powerful tools for businesses looking to showcase their products, demonstrate tutorials, or create educational content. By utilizing YouTube's targeting options, businesses can reach their target audience based on demographics, interests, or even specific videos or channels they are watching.

Optimizing PPC Campaigns:

To maximize the effectiveness of PPC campaigns, businesses should continuously monitor and optimize their strategies. By analyzing key metrics such as click-through rates, conversion rates, and return on ad spend, businesses can make data-driven decisions and refine their campaigns accordingly. This continuous refinement takes into account platform changes, industry trends, and consumer behavior.

Businesses can experiment with different targeting options, ad creatives, and bidding strategies to find the most effective combination. A/B testing can be performed to compare the performance of different ad variations and make informed decisions based on real-time data. Additionally, using conversion tracking tools helps businesses understand the customer journey, measure the effectiveness of their campaigns, and identify areas for improvement.

In conclusion, PPC advertising provides businesses with a powerful tool to reach their target audience, drive traffic, and generate conversions. By utilizing platforms such as Facebook Ads, Google Ads, LinkedIn Ads, Instagram Ads, and YouTube Ads, businesses can effectively engage with their audience and achieve their marketing objectives. However, it is crucial to stay up-to-date with platform changes, industry trends, and consumer behavior to continuously refine and evolve PPC strategies for optimal results in the ever-changing digital marketing landscape.

7

Social Media Marketing: Engaging and Connecting with Your Audience

In today's digital age, social media has become an integral part of our lives. It has not only transformed the way we connect and communicate with each other but has also revolutionized the way businesses interact with their audience. Social media platforms such as Facebook, LinkedIn, Instagram, Google, YouTube, and Twitter have provided businesses with unprecedented opportunities to engage and connect with their target audience like never before.

1. Understanding Your Target Audience: To effectively engage and connect with your audience on social media, you must first understand who they are. Conduct thorough market research to identify your target audience's demographics, interests, preferences, and online behavior. This knowledge will help you tailor your social media marketing efforts to resonate with your audience and capture their attention.

Facebook, with over 2.8 billion monthly active users, offers unparalleled reach and diverse demographics. It provides businesses with various features such as groups, pages, and ads to engage with their audience effectively. Facebook allows businesses to target specific audiences based on location, age, gender, interests, and more, ensuring that your content reaches the right people.

LinkedIn, the world's leading professional networking platform, attracts over 740 million professionals globally. It is an ideal platform for B2B marketing, networking, and showcasing thought leadership through industry-related content. LinkedIn offers business pages, groups, and targeted advertising options that allow you to connect with professionals in your industry and establish your brand as an authority.

Instagram, known for its visually appealing nature, has more than 1 billion active monthly users. Its focus on visual content makes it perfect for businesses in industries such as fashion, food, travel, and lifestyle. Instagram offers features like Stories, IGTV, and Reels that allow businesses to showcase their products or services creatively and engage their audience through captivating visuals.

Google, primarily known as a search engine, also offers social media features such as Google My Business and Google Plus. These platforms allow businesses to engage with their audience through reviews, posts, and updates, enhancing their online presence. Google My Business allows you to display essential information like address, phone number, and business hours, improving your visibility in local searches.

YouTube, the world's largest video-sharing platform, boasts over 2 billion monthly active users. Businesses can leverage YouTube to showcase their expertise, reach a vast audience, and engage with their audience through video content, tutorials, testimonials, and brand stories. YouTube provides monetization options, allowing businesses to earn revenue from advertising and sponsored videos.

Twitter, with its real-time and quick-sharing nature, has approximately 330 million monthly active users. It is ideal for businesses that want to engage with their audience through short and concise messages or participate in trending conversations. Twitter allows businesses to track hashtags, respond to customer queries, and build brand awareness through Twitter ads.

2. Selecting the Right Social Media Channels:

Not all social media platforms are created equal, and not every platform may be relevant to your business. Evaluate your target audience's preferences and the nature of your business to determine which social media channels will be the most effective in reaching and engaging your audience. Consider factors such as the platform's user base, features, and the type of content that performs well on each channel.

For example, if you're targeting a younger demographic, platforms like Instagram and TikTok might be more suitable due to their visual appeal and popularity among this age group. On the other hand, LinkedIn might be the better choice for B2B businesses looking to connect with professionals and establish thought leadership.

Additionally, consider emerging and niche social media platforms specific to your industry. For instance, Pinterest is popular for DIY, cooking, and fashion content, while Twitch is a live-streaming platform often used by gamers and e-sports enthusiasts.

Regardless of the platforms you choose, it is essential to maintain a consistent brand presence across all channels. This coherence ensures that your audience can recognize and connect with your brand, regardless of the platform they are using.

3. Crafting Engaging Content:

Once you've identified the right social media channels for your business, it's time to create compelling and engaging content that resonates with your audience. Whether it's informative blog posts, visually appealing images, entertaining videos, or thought-provoking infographics, your content should be tailored to the preferences and interests of your audience. Don't be afraid to experiment with different formats and styles to see what resonates the most with your audience.

Facebook offers various types of content, such as text posts, images, videos, live streams, and polls. Using a mix of these formats can keep your audience engaged and interested in your brand. Experiment with different types of content to see which ones generate the most interaction and engagement.

LinkedIn's professional environment lends itself well to educational resources, industry insights, industry news, and thought leadership articles.

Share content that adds value to your audience's professional development and stimulates meaningful discussions. Long-form articles and thought-provoking discussions are particularly effective on this platform.

Instagram's visual-centric platform requires eye-catching imagery, attention-grabbing captions, and strategic use of hashtags. Consider using Instagram Stories, Highlights, and Reels to enhance your engagement and storytelling. Use high-quality visuals that align with your brand's aesthetic and connect with your audience emotionally.

On Google, ensure your Google My Business profile is updated with relevant information and engaging posts. Utilize Google Plus for sharing valuable content, connecting with industry communities, and enhancing search engine visibility. Share blog posts, news updates, and industry insights to position yourself as an authoritative source.

YouTube's video-centric platform provides an excellent opportunity to showcase your expertise, product demonstrations, tutorials, and engaging storytelling. Invest in high-quality video production to ensure your content stands out. Optimize your videos with relevant keywords and engaging thumbnails to increase their visibility on YouTube and search engines.

Twitter's character limit challenges businesses to convey messages concisely. Use hashtags, impactful visuals, and engage in real-time conversations to draw attention to your brand or participate in trending topics. Create tweets that provoke discussion, ask questions, or make bold statements to encourage engagement. Utilize Twitter's multimedia features, such as GIFs and videos, to make your content more captivating.

4. Building a Community:

Social media is not just about broadcasting your message; it's about building a community of loyal followers who are actively engaged with your brand. Encourage your audience to like, comment, and share your posts, and take the time to respond to their comments and messages promptly. Foster meaningful conversations, ask for feedback, and show genuine interest in your audience's thoughts and opinions. By building a community, you create a sense of belonging and loyalty among your audience, which can lead to long-term success.

Utilize Facebook groups to create a space for your audience to interact with each other and your brand. Encourage discussions, share exclusive content, and ask for feedback to create a sense of community. Actively participate in conversations and respond to comments to foster a sense of belonging and build trust.

LinkedIn Groups provide professionals with a platform to discuss industry-related topics and connect. Join relevant groups in your industry and actively contribute to discussions. Share valuable insights, answer questions, and engage with other group members to establish yourself as an authority and build meaningful relationships.

Engage with relevant industry hashtags on Instagram to join conversations and encourage user-generated content. Show appreciation for user-generated content by reposting and giving credit. Encourage your audience toengage with your brand by running contests, challenges, or giveaways that require user participation. This can help create a sense of community and encourage your audience to actively engage with your content.

On Google, respond to reviews and interact with customers who leave feedback. Address any concerns or issues promptly and professionally, showing your commitment to customer satisfaction. Use Google My Business posts to share updates, news, and promotions, and encourage customers to leave reviews and share their experiences.

YouTube allows for comments on videos, so make sure to respond to comments and engage with your viewers. Encourage viewers to subscribe to your channel and turn on notifications for new content. Host live streams or Q&A sessions to directly interact with your audience and answer their questions.

Twitter's real-time nature makes it conducive for engaging in conversations and joining trending topics. Monitor relevant hashtags and mentions of your brand, and respond to comments and inquiries in a timely manner. Retweet and engage with your followers' content to show appreciation and build a sense of community.

5. Utilizing Social Media Advertising:

In addition to organic efforts, social media advertising can significantly boost your reach and engagement with your target audience. Each social media platform offers advertising options and targeting tools that allow you to reach specific segments of your audience with tailored messages.

Facebook Ads Manager provides businesses with a comprehensive advertising platform, allowing you to create and manage ads easily. You can set specific objectives, determine your target audience, and customize your ad formats. Utilize Facebook's targeting options to reach specific demographics, interests, and behaviors. Experiment with different ad formats, such as image ads, video ads, carousel ads, and messenger ads, to see which ones resonate best with your audience.

LinkedIn offers a native advertising platform called LinkedIn Campaign Manager, which allows you to create and launch text ads, sponsored content, and messaging ads. You can target your ads based on job titles, industries, company sizes, and more. Consider using LinkedIn's Lead Gen Forms to capture leads directly on the platform, making it easier for your audience to engage with your offers.

Instagram offers various advertising options, including photo ads, video ads, carousel ads, and story ads. Utilize Instagram's targeting features to reach your desired audience based on demographics, interests, behaviors, and more. Instagram also allows for influencer collaborations, where you partner with popular Instagram accounts to promote your products or services.

Google Ads enables businesses to run ads across Google's vast network, including search ads, display ads, video ads, and app ads. Utilize Google's targeting options to reach your target audience based on keywords, demographics, interests, and more. Take advantage of remarketing campaigns to target users who have previously interacted with your website or app.

YouTube offers various advertising options, including in-stream ads, video discovery ads, bumper ads, and masthead ads. Target your ads based on demographics, interests, keywords, and placements to reach your desired audience. YouTube also offers advanced targeting options, such as affinity targeting, life events targeting, and custom intent targeting.

Twitter Ads allows businesses to promote tweets, accounts, and trends to engage with their audience. Utilize Twitter's targeting options, such as keywords, interests, followers, and demographics, to reach your desired audience. Experiment with different ad formats, including promoted tweets, promoted accounts, and promoted trends, to see what generates the best engagement.

Engaging and connecting with your audience on social media requires a comprehensive strategy that involves understanding your target audience, selecting the right social media channels, crafting engaging content, building a community, and utilizing social media advertising. By effectively utilizing these strategies, you can establish a strong online presence, build meaningful relationships with your audience, and drive business growth through social media marketing. Remember to consistently monitor and analyze your social media efforts, adjusting your strategy as needed to ensure ongoing success.

8

The Power of Influencer Marketing

In today's hyperconnected world, where social media has become an integral part of our daily lives, influencer marketing has emerged as a powerful strategy for brands to connect with their target audience. As consumers become increasingly resistant to traditional forms of advertising, influencer marketing offers a way to tap into the trust and influence that social media personalities have built.

Understanding the core principles of influencer marketing is essential for brands looking to leverage the potential of this strategy. It begins with the identification of the right influencers for your brand. It's not solely about the number of followers an influencer has, but more about the quality of their engagement. Micro-influencers, for example, may have smaller followings but boast highly engaged communities, where individuals feel a genuine connection with the influencer. This authenticity and engagement can translate into a more meaningful impact when it comes to promoting your brand.

When selecting influencers, it is crucial to find individuals aligned with your target audience and whose values and content resonate with your brand message. The influencer's audience should closely match your ideal customer profile to ensure that your collaboration reaches the right people. Through these carefully chosen influencers, brands can tap into established communities that trust and value the opinions of their favorite social media personalities.

Building a strong relationship with influencers is a crucial step in successful influencer marketing. It involves more than a simple transactional partnership; it requires genuine interest and active communication. Approaching influencers with respect and acknowledging their work fosters trust and opens the door to long-term partnerships. By facilitating genuine connections with influencers, brands can create authentic campaigns that resonate with the audience and deliver impactful results.

Now, let's explore the different types of influencer collaborations in more detail. The first type is product sponsorships, where influencers showcase your product in their content. This collaboration works well when you want to create awareness and generate interest in a specific product. It's essential to ensure that the influencer's audience aligns with your target market, and the product integrates seamlessly into the influencer's content, making it feel natural and authentic.

The second type is sponsored posts, where influencers create dedicated content to promote your brand or a specific campaign. This can take various forms such as blog posts, YouTube videos, or Instagram stories. Sponsored posts provide influencers with creative freedom to craft narratives that resonate with their audience while subtly incorporating your brand or campaign message. Striking the right balance between authentic storytelling and promotional content is crucial to maintain the influencer's credibility and engagement levels.

Lastly, there are ambassador programs, which involve forming long-term partnerships with influencers who become brand advocates. Selecting influencers who align closely with your brand values and vision allows for a more meaningful connection to develop. These ambassadors are passionate about your brand and invest in consistently promoting your products over an extended period. The trust and credibility they build with their followers can significantly impact your brand's perception and ultimately drive sales.

While influencer marketing can amplify your brand's visibility and reach, it is important to approach it with a strategic mindset. Transparent communication, clear goals, and measurable KPIs are vital for evaluating the success of your influencer campaigns. It enables you to track engagement, reach, and conversion rates to gain valuable insights into the impact of your partnerships. This data-driven approach allows for continuous refinement of your influencer marketing strategy, ensuring that it stays aligned with your overall business objectives and delivers measurable results.

In conclusion, influencer marketing is a dynamic and rapidly evolving strategy that offers brands an opportunity to connect with their target audience in an authentic and influential way. By collaborating with carefully selected influencers, you can tap into their established communities and leverage their trust and expertise to promote your brand effectively. However, success in influencer marketing requires strategic planning, relationship building, and a commitment to creating meaningful and engaging content. Embrace the power of influencer marketing and witness its transformative impact on your brand's growth and success in the digital landscape.

9

Content Marketing: Storytelling in the Digital Age

Content marketing has become a powerful tool in the digital age, allowing businesses to connect with their audience on a deeper level. In this chapter, we will explore the art of storytelling and how it can be leveraged to create compelling content that resonates with your target audience.

Clients need to be able to relate to you:

In today's competitive marketplace, building strong relationships with clients is crucial for success. Customers want to connect with businesses on a personal level and feel understood. When clients are able to relate to you and your brand's story, they are more likely to trust and engage with your content. By leveraging the power of storytelling in your content marketing strategy, you can ensure that your clients see themselves in your brand's narrative, fostering a sense of authenticity and building long-lasting connections.

Understanding the Power of Storytelling:

In the digital landscape, consumers are constantly bombarded with information from various sources. To capture their attention, it is essential to cut through the noise and engage them emotionally. Storytelling has the power to do just that. When you tell a story, you create a personal connection with your audience by evoking emotions and sparking their imagination. Storytelling is not just about conveying facts; it is about creating an experience that resonates with your audience on an emotional level. By weaving narratives into your content, you can make your brand more relatable and memorable, leaving a lasting impact on your clients.

Defining Your Brand Narrative:
To effectively incorporate storytelling into your content marketing efforts, it is crucial to identify and define your brand narrative. Your brand narrative encompasses the story behind your brand, including its origins, values, mission, and unique selling proposition. It is the thread that weaves all your content together and helps consumers understand who you are as a brand. By understanding and articulating your brand narrative, you can create a consistent and authentic storytelling foundation to guide your content creation process. This cohesive narrative allows your clients to better understand your brand's purpose and values, generating trust and loyalty.

Tailoring Your Content to Your Audience:
Effective content marketing is not just about telling stories; it's about understanding your audience and crafting content that resonates with them. To create content that engages and connects, you must dive deeply into your target audience's demographics, preferences, and pain points. By conducting thorough market research and developing accurate buyer personas, you can gain valuable insights into your audience's needs, desires, and motivations. Armed with this knowledge, you can create content that speaks directly to your clients, addressing their challenges and offering solutions that they can relate to. The more specific and tailored your storytelling is to your audience, the more impactful it will be.

Building a Storytelling Framework:
To consistently deliver engaging and compelling content, it is essential to

establish a storytelling framework. This framework serves as a roadmap for creating content aligned with your brand narrative and overall storytelling goals. It defines the key elements of your brand's story, including characters, plotlines, themes, and messages. It helps you to create a cohesive and consistent narrative across all your content channels. By having a well-defined structure, you can ensure consistency in your messaging and maintain a cohesive brand story. This consistency enhances your client's ability to connect with your brand and builds a strong foundation for long-term relationships.

Leveraging Different Content Formats:

In the digital age, content comes in various formats, each with its own unique advantages and challenges. To maximize your reach and engage different segments of your audience, it is crucial to leverage multiple content formats. Some clients may prefer written content like blog posts and articles, while others may be more receptive to visual content like videos or infographics. By experimenting with different mediums and tailoring your storytelling approach to suit each format, you can create a diverse content ecosystem that captivates and engages your audience across various channels. The more versatile and adaptive your storytelling is, the wider your audience reach will be.

Measuring the Impact of Your Content Marketing Efforts:

No content marketing strategy is complete without measuring its impact and effectiveness. To continuously improve your storytelling techniques and optimize your content, it is essential to track key metrics related to your marketing efforts. These metrics may include website traffic, social media engagement, lead generation, conversion rates, and customer satisfaction. By analyzing these metrics, you can gain valuable insights into the success of your content, make data-driven decisions, and refine your storytelling strategies to better resonate with your clients. Measuring the impact of your content marketing efforts allows you to focus on what works and adapt your storytelling techniques accordingly.

In conclusion, storytelling in content marketing allows businesses to connect with their audience on a deeper level, fostering relationships built on trust and authenticity. By understanding the power of storytelling, defining your brand narrative, tailoring content to your audience, building a storytelling framework, leveraging different content formats, and measuring the impact of your efforts, you can create a compelling and impactful content marketing strategy that sets you apart in the digital age. By allowing your clients to relate to you and your brand's story, you create a bond of trust and understanding that can lead to long-term success. Remember, clients need to be able to relate to you, and storytelling is the perfect tool to make that happen.

10

Email Marketing: Nurturing and Retaining Customers

In today's digital landscape, email marketing has become an essential tool for nurturing and retaining customers. It provides businesses with a direct and personalized way to communicate with their audience, build trust, and ultimately drive sales. In this chapter, we will explore the strategies and techniques to effectively use email marketing to nurture and retain customers.

In order to retain customers, you have to build trust:

Building trust is a fundamental step in retaining customers. Without trust, customers are unlikely to engage with your brand and may even unsubscribe from your email list. Trust can be established through various means, including:

Transparency: Be open and honest with your customers about your business practices, pricing, and any potential drawbacks. Transparency builds credibility and instills confidence in your brand.

Consistent Branding: Maintain a consistent brand image across all your email communication. This ensures that customers can easily recognize and identify with your brand, establishing familiarity and trust.

Authenticity: Be genuine and authentic in your email communication. Avoid using overly sales-y or promotional language. Instead, focus on building real connections with your audience by sharing valuable and meaningful content.

Customer Testimonials: Showcase positive feedback and testimonials from satisfied customers. This social proof helps to build trust and reinforces the credibility of your brand.

GDPR Compliance: Ensure that your email marketing practices are in compliance with privacy regulations, such as the General Data Protection Regulation (GDPR). By respecting your customers' privacy and protecting their data, you establish trust and demonstrate your commitment to their well-being.

Now, let's delve deeper into the strategies and techniques for nurturing and retaining customers through email marketing:

Personalize the Email Content:

Personalization is key to making customers feel valued and understood. People receive numerous emails every day, and generic messages are often ignored. By segmenting your email list based on demographics, past purchases, or engagement levels, businesses can deliver targeted and personalized content that resonates with each customer segment. This could include personalized product recommendations, relevant offers, or exclusive content. The more tailored your emails are, the more likely customers are to engage and see the value in your communication.

Provide Value:

Customers are more likely to stay connected with a brand when they consistently receive value from their emails. To retain customers, businesses should focus on offering useful tips, educational content, or exclusive discounts that are relevant to their interests and preferences. By providing valuable content, businesses not only keep customers engaged but also position themselves as a trusted source of information in their industry. This added value strengthens the customer's perception of your brand and encourages them to remain engaged with your emails.

Segment and Target:

Not all customers are the same, and sending a generic email blast to everyone on your list is unlikely to yield results. By segmenting your email list based on various criteria such as demographics, past purchases, or engagement levels, you can deliver targeted and more relevant content that resonates with each customer segment. This targeted approach demonstrates that you understand your customers' specific needs and preferences, fostering a sense of trust and loyalty. Additionally, segmenting allows you to tailor your messaging to address specific pain points or address the needs of your customers at different stages of their journey.

Automate Email Campaigns:

Automation tools allow businesses to set up email campaigns that are triggered by specific customer actions or events. By automating certain aspects of your email marketing, you can ensure that customers receive timely and relevant messages, increasing the chances of engagement and retention. For example, sending a welcome email to new subscribers or following up with customers who have abandoned their shopping carts can help nurture relationships and encourage repeat purchases. Automation streamlines your efforts and ensures that your customers receive consistent and timely communication, strengthening their connection to your brand.

Encourage Engagement and Feedback:

Active engagement from customers is crucial for building trust and improving the effectiveness of email marketing campaigns. Encourage customers to provide feedback, respond to their inquiries promptly, and make it easy for them to engage with your brand. This can be done through clear call-to-actions, interactive content, and personalized responses. By actively engaging with customers, businesses can foster a sense of trust and show customers that their opinions and feedback are valued. Additionally, providing opportunities for customers to engage with your brand, such as through surveys, contests, or social media, can contribute to building a more robust and loyal customer base.

Monitor and Analyze Results:

To continually improve your email marketing efforts, it is important to monitor key metrics such as open rates, click-through rates, and conversion rates. Analyzing this data will offer valuable insights into the performance of your campaigns and help you make strategic improvements. By continually monitoring and optimizing your email marketing strategy, you can ensure that you are nurturing and retaining customers effectively. Regularly evaluating and analyzing the results of your campaigns allows you to identify strengths, weaknesses, and areas for improvement. This data-driven approach enables you to make informed decisions and refine your email marketing strategy to better cater to the needs and expectations of your customers.

Remember, email marketing is a long-term relationship-building strategy. By consistently providing value, personalizing content, and fostering engagement, businesses can nurture and retain their customers, ultimately leading to increased customer loyalty and sales. Building trust through personalized and valuable email marketing campaigns is a crucial component of successful customer retention.

11

Analytics and Reporting: Measuring and Improving Digital Marketing Efforts

In today's digital landscape, data has become a powerful tool for marketers to understand their audience, measure the success of their campaigns, and make informed decisions to optimize their digital marketing efforts. This chapter delves deeper into the topic of analytics and reporting, exploring the features and benefits of various tools such as Google Analytics, Facebook Insights, LinkedIn Analytics, and YouTube Analytics.

Google Analytics

Google Analytics is one of the most widely used analytics tools, providing marketers with a comprehensive view of website traffic, user behavior, and conversions. With its robust set of features, Google Analytics allows marketers to track various metrics, identify valuable insights, and optimize their marketing strategies.

Website Traffic Analysis: Google Analytics provides an overview of the number of visitors to a website, with the ability to segment the data by various dimensions such as location, demographics, and traffic sources. Marketers can gain insights into which channels or campaigns are driving the most traffic, enabling them to allocate their resources efficiently.

Additionally, Google Analytics offers a feature called "Acquisition" that allows marketers to delve deeper into their website traffic sources. This feature provides insight into which channels are driving the most traffic, such as organic search, paid search, social media, referrals, or direct traffic. By understanding the source of traffic, marketers can focus their efforts on channels that are generating the most valuable visitors.

User Behavior Insights: Understanding user behavior on a website is crucial for optimizing digital marketing efforts. Google Analytics offers metrics such as bounce rate, average session duration, and page views. By analyzing these metrics, marketers can identify areas of improvement to enhance user experience and drive conversions.

Google Analytics also provides data on user flow, which shows the path users take through a website, including the pages they visit and where they drop off. This information helps marketers identify any bottlenecks or points of friction in the conversion funnel, allowing them to optimize the user journey and increase conversion rates.

Conversion Tracking: Conversion tracking is a vital aspect of measuring the effectiveness of digital marketing efforts. Google Analytics enables marketers to set up goals and track conversions, such as completing a purchase, submitting a lead form, or signing up for a newsletter. This data allows marketers to identify high-performing campaigns and optimize underperforming ones.

Furthermore, Google Analytics offers the option to set up e-commerce tracking. This feature allows marketers to track the revenue generated from online sales, the products or services that generate the most revenue, and the average order value. By understanding the performance of specific products or services, marketers can tweak their marketing strategies to maximize sales and overall revenue.

Social Media Analytics

Social media platforms provide their own analytics tools that offer insights into audience demographics, engagement, and reach. Let's take a closer look at the analytics features of Facebook Insights, LinkedIn Analytics, and YouTube Analytics.

Facebook Insights:

Facebook Insights offers valuable data for marketers managing Facebook Pages. It provides metrics on audience demographics, reach, engagement, and post-performance, enabling marketers to analyze the success of their content strategy. Marketers can track page likes, post engagement and even run A/B tests to optimize their content.

In addition to these metrics, Facebook Insights also provides the option to analyze the performance of live videos. Marketers can monitor metrics such as concurrent viewers, peak live viewers, and reactions, allowing them to assess the effectiveness of their live video content and make improvements for future broadcasts.

LinkedIn Analytics:

For professionals and B2B marketers, LinkedIn Analytics is a valuable tool for understanding page performance and engagement metrics. It offers insights into the reach, impressions, and engagement of company pages. LinkedIn Analytics provides valuable data on follower demographics, allowing marketers to tailor their messaging and content strategy accordingly.

LinkedIn Analytics also provides data on the performance of individual LinkedIn posts. Marketers can analyze metrics such as clicks, likes, comments, and shares to determine the popularity and relevance of their content. By understanding which posts resonate most with their audience, marketers can refine their content strategy and increase engagement.

YouTube Analytics:

YouTube Analytics provides in-depth metrics related to video performance on the platform. Marketers can access data on views, watch time, audience retention, and engagement metrics like likes, comments, and shares. This information helps marketers understand which videos are resonating with their audience and optimize their content strategy for maximum impact.

Beyond these metrics, YouTube Analytics offers demographic data on the audience watching the videos, including age, gender, and geographic location. Marketers can use this data to target specific demographics with their video content and tailor their messaging to the preferences and interests of their audience.

Advertising Platform Analytics

Digital advertising platforms like Google Ads and Facebook Ads Manager also offer comprehensive analytics and reporting features. These platforms enable marketers to track key performance indicators (KPIs) and optimize their ad campaigns effectively.

Google Ads:

With Google Ads, marketers can access detailed reporting on metrics such as impressions, click-through rates (CTRs), conversions, and cost per acquisition (CPA). Additionally, Google Ads provides features like A/B testing to optimize ad copy, imagery, and targeting parameters, helping marketers maximize their ROI.

Google Ads also offers advanced features such as remarketing and audience segmentation. Marketers can analyze the performance of different audience segments and adjust their campaign targeting to drive better results. By leveraging these features, marketers can further optimize their advertising campaigns and increase their conversion rates.

Facebook Ads Manager:

Facebook Ads Manager provides insights into ad campaign performance across the Facebook platform, including Facebook, Instagram, and Audience Network. Marketers can analyze metrics such as impressions, reach, click-through rates (CTRs), and ad engagement. The platform allows for A/B testing and optimization to drive better results.

In addition to these metrics, Facebook Ads Manager offers features like custom audience targeting and lookalike audience creation. Marketers can analyze the performance of different audience segments and leverage lookalike audiences to expand their reach to users who share similar characteristics to their existing customer base. These features enhance the effectiveness of Facebook advertising campaigns and increase the likelihood of reaching and engaging the target audience.

Marketing Automation and Attribution Modeling

In addition to individual platform analytics, marketers can leverage marketing automation tools that offer comprehensive reporting features to track and measure various marketing channels in one place. These tools provide a holistic view of campaign performance and aid marketers in making data-driven decisions.

Marketing Automation Tools:

Marketing automation tools like HubSpot, Marketo, or Mailchimp offer robust analytics and reporting capabilities. These platforms allow marketers to track key metrics across different channels, including email marketing, social media, and content marketing. Centralized reporting facilitates better visibility and analysis of campaigns, enabling marketers to make informed decisions.

In addition to reporting features, marketing automation tools often offer advanced features like lead scoring and nurturing, which help marketers better understand their leads' behavior and tailor their messaging to drive conversions. By utilizing these features, marketers can increase the efficiency of their lead generation and nurturing efforts, resulting in higher conversion rates.

Attribution Modeling:

Attribution modeling is a technique that helps marketers understand the customer journey and the impact of different touchpoints on conversions. Advanced marketing automation tools often include attribution modeling capabilities, which allow marketers to assign values to various marketing channels and assess their contribution to conversions. This information enables marketers to optimize their budget allocation and focus on high-performing channels.

There are different types of attribution models, such as first touch, last touch, linear, and time decay. Each model has its pros and cons, and marketers can choose the model that best aligns with their marketing goals and strategies. By leveraging attribution modeling, marketers can gain a better understanding of the effectiveness of their marketing efforts, identify which channels are driving the most conversions, and optimize their campaigns accordingly. This data-driven approach helps marketers allocate their budget more effectively and maximize their return on investment (ROI).

Reporting and Insights

Effective reporting is essential for measuring the success of digital marketing efforts and communicating the results to stakeholders. Here are some best practices for reporting and gaining insights from analytics data:

Define KPIs: Clearly define the key performance indicators (KPIs) that align with your marketing goals. This could include metrics like website traffic, conversions, engagement, or revenue. Having well-defined KPIs will help you focus on the metrics that are most relevant to your objectives.

Set up Custom Dashboards: Many analytics tools offer the option to create custom dashboards, allowing you to organize and visualize the data that matters most to you. Custom dashboards can help you track and monitor your KPIs in real-time, making it easier to identify trends, anomalies, and areas for improvement.

Regularly Analyze and Review Data: It's important to regularly analyze your analytics data and review your performance. Set aside dedicated time to review your metrics, compare them against your goals, and identify any patterns or insights that can inform your marketing strategies.

Create Actionable Insights: Turn your data into actionable insights by identifying opportunities for improvement. For example, if you notice a high bounce rate on a specific landing page, you can investigate the issue and make changes to improve user experience and increase conversions.

Experiment and Test: Use A/B testing or multi-variate testing to try out different elements of your marketing campaigns and measure the impact on your KPIs. This iterative approach allows you to continuously optimize your strategies based on data-driven insights.

Create Comprehensive Reports: When presenting your insights and results to stakeholders, create comprehensive reports that include key metrics, trends, and actionable recommendations. Use visuals, charts, and graphs to make the data more digestible and understandable.

Continuously Learn and Improve: Digital marketing is always evolving, so it's crucial to stay updated on industry trends, emerging technologies, and new strategies. Continuously learning and adapting based on insights and new information will help you stay ahead and improve your digital marketing efforts over time.

In conclusion, analytics and reporting play a critical role in measuring and improving digital marketing efforts. By utilizing tools like Google Analytics, social media analytics, advertising platform analytics, marketing automation, and attribution modeling, marketers can gather valuable insights, optimize their campaigns, and make data-driven decisions. Regular analysis, reporting, and experimentation are vital for continuous improvement and achieving marketing goals in the ever-changing digital landscape.

12

The Future of Digital Marketing

As we embark on the journey into the future, it is crucial to understand the evolving landscape of digital marketing. The relentless pace of technological advancements has led to significant changes in the way businesses connect with consumers. In this chapter, we will explore the exciting possibilities and potential challenges that lie ahead in the world of digital marketing.

One of the most evident trends shaping the future of digital marketing is the increasing integration of artificial intelligence (AI) and machine learning. AI-powered algorithms can now analyze vast amounts of data, allowing marketers to gain deeper insights into consumer behavior and preferences. These advancements enable personalized marketing experiences that were once unimaginable. By leveraging AI, marketers can create targeted advertisements, tailored product recommendations, and customized messaging to enhance user engagement and conversion rates.

The use of AI in digital marketing goes beyond just data analysis. Chatbots, powered by AI, have revolutionized customer service in the digital realm. With advancements in natural language processing (NLP), chatbots can now provide instant, personalized assistance, solving customer queries and offering recommendations. Not only do chatbots enhance customer satisfaction, but they also help businesses gather valuable data about customer preferences and pain points, enabling them to refine their marketing strategies. This efficient and cost-effective solution allows businesses to handle a large volume of customer inquiries without compromising the quality of service.

Furthermore, AI algorithms can be used to automate repetitive tasks, freeing up marketers to focus on strategy and creativity. From content creation to ad optimization, AI-powered tools can assist marketers in improving efficiency and reducing manual labor. For instance, AI can intelligently analyze data to determine the best times and platforms to reach a target audience, as well as optimize ad campaigns in real-time based on user responses.

In the realm of search engine optimization (SEO), voice-based search and smart devices are becoming integral parts of our daily lives. With the rise of virtual assistants like Siri, Alexa, and Google Assistant, people are now using voice commands to search for information, make purchases, and control their smart home devices. Voice search requires a different approach to traditional keyword-based searches, as it often involves long-tail conversational queries. As a savvy marketer, it is vital to optimize your content for voice search by incorporating natural, conversational language and answering common questions that users may ask.

Additionally, local SEO becomes even more critical for voice-based searches, as users often seek immediate information and recommendations based on their location. Marketers must ensure their business information is accurately listed in online directories and review platforms to appear in relevant local searches. Collaboration with local influencers and leveraging location-specific content can also help boost visibility and engagement.

Social media platforms continue to thrive and evolve, creating new opportunities for digital marketers. The power of influencer marketing has become evident, as consumers are more likely to trust recommendations from individuals they admire and follow. Engaging with influencers can help brands create authentic connections with their target audience, building trust and credibility. However, as social media algorithms constantly change, marketers must stay agile and adapt their strategies to ensure maximum visibility and engagement.

Creating shareable content is essential to encourage organic reach and user-generated content. Engaging with your audience and encouraging them to create and share content related to your brand can significantly expand your reach. User-generated content not only amplifies your brand message but also serves as social proof, boosting trust among potential customers.

In addition to organic reach, targeted advertising options on social media platforms provide a powerful way to connect with specific segments of your audience. Leveraging the data collected by these platforms, marketers can create highly targeted and personalized ad campaigns, reaching potential customers with precision. The ability to target users based on interests, demographics, and behavior gives businesses the opportunity to deliver relevant content and offers that resonate with their audience.

An area that holds tremendous potential for digital marketers is augmented reality (AR) and virtual reality (VR). These immersive technologies have the power to revolutionize the way consumers experience products and services. By blending the digital world with the real world, businesses can provide interactive and captivating experiences that drive brand engagement and increase sales. Imagine a customer being able to try on clothes virtually or visualize how furniture would look in their living room before making a purchase.

Incorporating AR and VR into digital marketing strategies can provide unique and memorable experiences that set a brand apart from the competition. This technology allows businesses to create a virtual showroom or interactive product demonstrations, enabling customers to fully experience and understand the features, benefits, and potential applications of a product or service.

With the increasing importance of data privacy and security, marketers must navigate the challenges of maintaining consumer trust. Stricter regulations and laws, such as the General Data Protection Regulation (GDPR), demand that businesses handle personal data responsibly. Marketers must ensure they collect and use customer data ethically, with transparent consent and proper security measures in place.

Adopting a customer-centric approach to data privacy can help build trust and foster long-term relationships with consumers. Clearly communicating your data collection practices, providing options for data control and consent, and keeping customers informed about how their data is being used can help establish a positive perception of your brand. Transparency builds trust and reassures customers that their privacy is a priority.

The future of digital marketing holds tremendous potential for innovation and growth. Marketers who embrace AI, optimize for voice search, leverage influencer marketing, explore AR and VR, and prioritize data privacy will be well-positioned to succeed in this ever-evolving landscape. However, it is crucial for marketers to stay updated with the latest trends and technologies, continually adapt their strategies, and foster creativity and agility in their approach.

As we move forward, the digital marketing landscape will continue to evolve, presenting both challenges and opportunities for those willing to embrace change and push the boundaries of what is possible. By staying informed, experimenting with new tools and techniques, and always putting the customer first, digital marketers can unlock the full potential of this ever-expanding digital world.

If you are interested in learning more about digital marketing, check out The Roadmap, the ultimate digital marketing course to generate low-maintenance income through social media at:

https://stan.store/TheDigitalPalette/p/roadmap-hh08